Herefordshire

Roy Woodcock

COUNTRYSIDE BOOKS
NEWBURY BERKSHIRE

First Published 2006
© Roy Woodcock, 2006

COUNTRYSIDE BOOKS
3 Catherine Road
Newbury, Berkshire

To view our complete range of books,
please visit us at
www.countrysidebooks.co.uk

ISBN 1 85306 981 7
EAN 978 1 85306 981 9

Cover picture is of Ross-on-Wye taken by Bill Meadows.

Photographs by the author
Designed by Peter Davies, Nautilus Design
Produced through MRM Associates Ltd, Reading
Printed by Woolnough Bookbinding Ltd., Irthlingborough

Contents

POCKET PUB WALKS

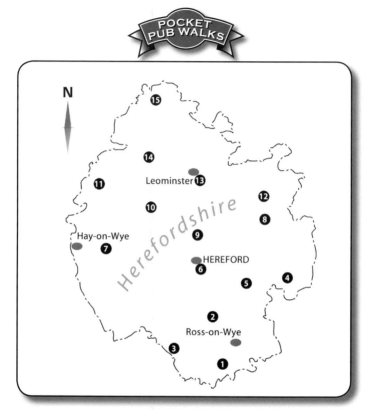

Area map showing location of the walks

Introduction

If you do not know the county of Herefordshire, it is time to come and pay a few visits – the countryside will delight and may surprise you. However, if you have been before there is much for you to revisit, and you will certainly be able to find and enjoy previously unknown locations.

The undulating landscape provides walks that may be steep or gentle, to suit all tastes. Shaped vaguely like a saucer, with the highest ground all around the edges, the county is bounded by the Malvern Hills in the east and the Black Mountains in the west, where the ridge reaches a height of 2,300 feet. The varied geology, much of Old Red Sandstone age, creates the undulating landscape of hills and vales. Rivers cross the county from the north and west towards the south and east, heading towards the Wye and the Severn on the way to the sea. In the north the River Arrow meets the Lugg and is joined by the Frome before reaching the Wye. The Leadon flows into the Severn and the Dore goes into the Monnow. These river valleys provide lowlands and gentle plains, with hills dotted here and there throughout the county. This collection, which is a purely subjective selection, visits a range of beautiful locations throughout the length and breadth of this rural county.

Herefordshire contains little industry, not many towns and very few people. The county population is about 170,000, with 65,000 of them living in the city of Hereford.

Architectural interest is widely found, with some buildings using local stone, whilst others are timber-framed black and white. Ancient settlements are dotted around the county, with old hill forts, Roman remains, and several castles guarding the Welsh Border. This is the Marches territory and remains of the Offa's Dyke can be seen in places.

A few of the traditional fields with hops, fruit trees or grazing cattle are still to be seen, but more varied crops as well as sheep are commoner nowadays. The growing of fruit, which gave rise to the brewing of beer, cider and perry, is still important so a good choice of local drinks can be easily found.

No county could be more attractive for the walker, with well-marked footpaths, not many people and glorious scenery. This book offers 15 varied circular routes, ranging in distance from 2½ to 6 miles, for a gentle half-day stroll, before or after a visit to a pub for lunch. I have included telephone numbers so that you can check opening hours and food serving times before you set out. Other features of interest near to the chosen pubs are also mentioned, for anyone intending to make a full day of it.

So, it just remains for me to wish you 'Happy Walking'!

Ray Wordeoch

Publisher's Note

We hope that you obtain considerable enjoyment from this book; great care has been taken in its preparation. However, changes of landlord and actual closures are sadly not uncommon. Likewise, although at the time of publication all routes followed public rights of way or permitted paths, diversion orders can be made and permissions withdrawn.

We cannot, of course, be held responsible for such diversion orders and any inaccuracies in the text which result from these or any other changes to the routes nor any damage which might result from walkers trespassing on private property. We are anxious though that all details covering the walks and pubs are kept up to date and would therefore welcome information from readers which would be relevant to future editions.

The simple sketch maps that accompany the walks in this book are based on notes made by the author whilst checking out the routes on the ground. However, for the benefit of a proper map, we do recommend that you purchase the relevant Ordnance Survey sheet covering your walk. The Ordnance Survey maps are widely available, especially through booksellers and local newsagents.

1 Goodrich & Coppett Hill

Ye Hostelrie Hotel

The village of Goodrich, with its Norman castle, is the start for this glorious Wye Valley walk. We start by climbing to the triangulation point on Coppett Hill with spectacular views all round, especially of the Wye. The hills of Wales and Shropshire can also be seen before a gentle descent leads us down to the road, through the churchyard and back into the village.

Distance – 3½ miles.

OS Explorer OL14 Wye Valley and Forest of Dean; **Landranger** 162 Gloucester and Forest of Dean. GR 576196.

Starting point The car park at Goodrich Castle.

How to get there *From the A40 Ross-on-Wye to Monmouth road, take any one of three roads to Goodrich. Follow signs to the castle where there is ample free parking. Alternatively, patrons may leave their cars in the pub car park (with permission) while they are walking.*

THE PUB The Goodrich village pub is **Ye Hostelrie Hotel**, a turreted folly of 1830, although parts date from 1625. The main road from London to South Wales passed by in the 16th and 17th centuries. It was a workhouse for a time in its early days but now offers comfortable accommodation. The bar and restaurant have a wide range of meals for all appetites, with an extensive à la carte menu in the restaurant, including speciality fish dishes. Outside there is a patio and garden, a real sun-trap in summer. Next door is the former resting place for monks on pilgrimage.
☎ *01600 890241; www.ye-hostelrie.co.uk*

1 From the **Goodrich Castle car park** walk back along the narrow road. If you have parked at **Ye Hostelrie Hotel**, turn left and pass the village hall. In either case, reach the centre of the village and the junction of roads. With the post office on the right there are two options ahead, the right fork passing the school. We take the left fork, signed to **Coppett Hill**, **Youth Hostel** (1½ miles), **Welsh Bicknor** and **Courtfield**. Begin to climb up this narrow road, passing over the **Dry Arch**, a high bridge with the road (B4229) to **Kerne Bridge** passing below. Views are already opening up, with **Goodrich church** and more of the village to the right, and the **River Wye** and **Kerne Bridge** to the left.

[2] When the narrow road splits, at a triangle of grass, our path is straight ahead, between the two roads, climbing steeply up into the woods. The ascent is helped by the series of steps, as we soon reach a few large lumps of sandstone with smooth pebbles embedded – the quartz conglomerate seen in many locations near **Symonds Yat**. Climb up on the clear path, through trees, then bracken and gorse to reach more open countryside. Views to the right, then to the left, and then back behind us, show rural landscapes and hills in all directions, with the **Black Mountains**, **Clee Hills**, **Malverns** and **Abberley** particularly prominent.

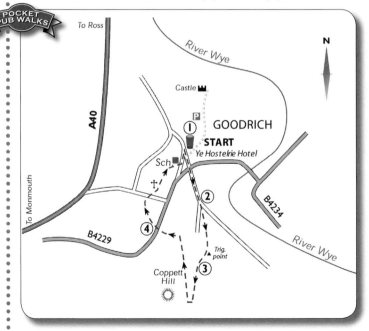

Herefordshire

Coppett Hill from the Symonds Yat Rock.

3 As we reach the top of the climb we find the triangulation point (188 m, 616 ft), and a few yards further on is the remnant of a ruined cottage - an 18th-century folly. Continue ahead now, on a fairly level path, with woods to the left and an open slope to the right. Descending slightly, reach a marker post and a crosspaths, which we ignore. But, after a further 50 yards where another broad grassy path leads off to the right, turn sharply here, and begin to descend through the bracken – with a line of telegraph poles close to the grassy path. As we descend, another path joins us from the left, but continue ahead to a stony track near the first houses. Keep straight ahead here across the track to a path descending through trees, with the gate of **High View** on our right. Descend to a T-junction and a track where we turn left and follow this down to the road.

Goodrich & Coppett Hill

4 Cross the road and, once through the wooden kissing gate, head diagonally right to the top corner of the field. Go on over a stile and up to the right corner of the next field, over the stile by the large gate, and walk along the track. This leads through to large houses and then a narrow road, where we turn right, passing **Granton House**, home of Joshua Cristall (1768–1847), the watercolour artist. Pass the **Vicarage** and then go left along the path to the large church of **St Giles** with its tall tower and broach spire, seen from a distance earlier in the walk. An interesting plan of the graves is shown in the porch, as well as a notice to say where the key can be borrowed (during shop hours). Walk through the churchyard to the old iron kissing gate in the bottom right hand corner, and out onto a path leading around the right margin of a field. Reach a metal kissing gate, and beyond here begin to descend, passing some trees planted by the children in the village school in 1997. Walk alongside the boundary fence of the modern school, and out to the road. Turn left here and pass the old school to reach the junction of roads we passed at the beginning of the walk.

Places of interest nearby

The red sandstone **Goodrich Castle,** built on a rocky outcrop, dates from the 12th and 13th centuries. It has many remains and rooms to explore, and the famous Roaring Meg (the gun that destroyed the castle) is on show. The last inhabitant was Charles I, during the Civil War.
☎ *01600 890538*

Symonds Yat Rock, 2 miles south of Goodrich, is an outcrop overlooking the Wye and is considered to have one of England's finest views. In summer, RSPB wardens will be able to point out the local peregrine falcon nest on nearby cliffs.

2 Hoarwithy

The New Harp Inn

Exploring a section of the beautiful Wye Valley, the walk takes us across fields, along the river bank and past (or visiting) three churches, showing English, Welsh and Italian influences. The attractive riverside village of Hoarwithy (the name is derived from an old name for whitebeam, or boundary willow) has houses dotted on the hillside all overlooked by the tower of the Italianate church of St Catherine, built of red sandstone in the 1880s around an existing chapel. J.P. Seddon

Distance – 5 miles.

OS Explorer 189 Hereford and Ross-on-Wye; **Landranger** 149 Hereford and Leominster, and just extending onto 162 Gloucester and the Forest of Dean. GR 546293.

Starting point The New Harp Inn in Hoarwithy.

How to get there Turn off the A49 Hereford to Ross-on-Wye road, along either one of two minor roads about 7 miles south of Hereford. The pub is on the roadside a little way to the south of the very prominent church tower. Patrons may park at the pub (with permission). Alternatively, you could leave your car in the lay-by near the river bridge at the northern end of the village.

was the architect, but ideas for the design came from the vicar of the time, William Poole.

THE PUB The **New Harp Inn** dates back to the 1880s, when the Old Harp was bought by two reverends who turned it into the Harp Temperance Hotel. So the owner, James Preece, moved to Fishbrook Cottage and started the New Harp. Recently refurbished after being damaged by fire, this picture-postcard pub serves delicious home-made food from a frequently changing menu. Meal selection can range from a sandwich to a three-course meal with fine wines. Specialities include Sunday lunches, for which booking is advisable. All visitors (and dogs) will find a warm welcome here. At the rear of the pub there is a decked patio and a garden crossed by a small stream.
☎ 01432 840900: www.newharpinn.co.uk

1 From the **New Harp** pub turn left and walk along the road, after admiring the old mill and garden opposite. After about

Herefordshire

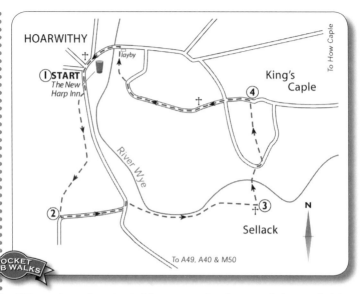

100 yards notice the bridleway, and a few yards beyond this, we fork diagonally to the right and up into the woods along a narrow path. Pass to the right of a house, then cross over a track and keep straight ahead on a narrow path. Reach an open field, go over the stile and walk alongside the hedge on the right. At the end of the field cross two stiles and a track, then bend right to walk along the top margin of the field. Continue over a stile by a large gate, onto a sunken track, with overhanging trees. The track leads out to a narrow road, on a bend, where we turn left.

2 Follow this road as it leads downhill to join a slightly bigger road. Go straight across the road, over the stile by the large gate, and follow the stony track. It curves right alongside the river bank. We soon pass a wooden hut, used by fishermen. Go through a gate or over the stile and continue to follow the river bank in this area of peace and tranquillity. Gradually begin to veer over

to the right towards the wooded slope (**Castlemeadow Wood**) and the far corner of the field. Go over the stile and turn right to the tiny hamlet of **Sellack**, and visit the **church of St Tysilio**, the only English church with this dedication. This sandstone church contains Norman as well as Victorian features.

3 From the church turn right and cross the field to the suspension bridge over the **River Wye**, which was built here in 1895, to replace the ferry. Once across the bridge in **Sellack Boat** – so named because there used to be the ferry crossing here – walk a few yards through trees to the road, and turn right. Pass a house on the right and then look for a stile in the hedge on the left.

The suspension bridge over the River Wye.

Herefordshire

Head straight across the field, to come alongside a hedge on the left. Climb steadily to a stile and on across a small field towards the right corner. Keep ahead over two stiles by metal gates, and walk along the driveway between houses, to reach the road.

4 Turn left and walk through **King's Caple**. Keep straight ahead at the crossroads and pass the village primary school and then the church – another sandstone church, with mounting steps on the roadside. The prominent spire was partially rebuilt in 1982. On the tump close by is the site of a Norman motte and bailey castle. Begin to descend and follow the narrow road, bending slightly to the right, and soon **Hoarwithy church** comes into view. When the road has a right-angled bend to the right, keep straight ahead along the green lane between hedges – descending. The path leads through to the road, at a layby (the alternative parking place) and here we turn left to cross over the **Wye**, on the bridge of 1990. The first bridge was built in 1856 and previously there was a ferry. It was a toll bridge until 1935 and the old toll house still survives at the end of the bridge. Notice the attractive houses up on the hillside to the right (looking almost alpine), as we follow the village street to reach the **New Harp**.

Places of interest nearby

How Caple Court Gardens, 5 miles east of Hoarwithy, are open from March to October. These 11-acre Edwardian gardens have formal terraces, informal areas of trees and shrubs, pools, a sunken Florentine garden and statues, and are set in glorious countryside with views extending to the Forest of Dean and the Welsh mountains.
☎ *01989 740626*

3 Garway

The Garway Moon Inn

Garway is set in stunning scenery, in a remote part of Herefordshire, in the hill country surrounding the **Monnow Valley.** The walk takes us from the village across the common, then down to the remarkable church noted for its origins and links with the **Knights Templars.** It continues along a lane lined with wild flowers and returns across meadows with sheep quietly grazing – an important feature of this hilly landscape.

Herefordshire

THE PUB The 16th century **Garway Moon Inn** still retains its flagstone floors, with stone walls and beamed ceilings, and serves a choice of home-made food. Also on offer are real ales including Wye Valley and other local brews. Children and walkers are welcome, and there is a beer garden and great views out across the common, where there is a children's playground and, in summer, you might find a cricket match in progress. The **Moon** is not always open at lunch time on weekdays in the winter, so it is advisable to check opening times.
☎ *01600 750270*

1 From the pub walk to the telephone box and turn right along the edge of the **common**. Follow the narrow road towards **Skenfrith**, passing between some houses and, when the road bends left, take the footpath straight ahead through the gate (with **Beechlands** painted on it). Follow the drive and, once beyond the house, turn right. The path passes through a gate and then alongside a hedge, with houses and gardens to the right. At the end of the field go over a stile and straight across

Distance – 3 miles.

OS Explorer 189 Hereford and Ross on Wye; **Landranger** 161 Abergavenny and the Black Mountains. GR 465227.

Starting point The Moon pub on the Common at Garway.

How to get there *Take the A466 north from Monmouth. After approximately 5 miles, turn left on the B4521 towards Abergavenny. At Broad Oak crossroads turn right, signed to Garway. Just over a mile along here reach the common and the pub. Park either alongside the common or in the pub car park, with permission.*

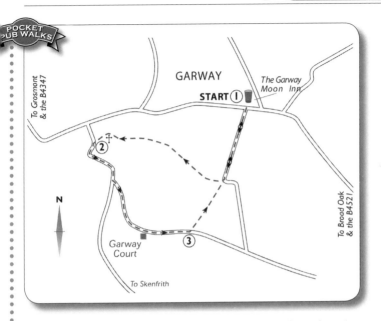

the next field, passing to the left of a telegraph pole and aiming towards the silo on the hill-top ahead. Go over another stile and, still keeping straight ahead, aim slightly to the left of the silo. The village can be seen away to the right as we cross the middle of this next field to reach another stile. From here there are good views down to the **church**, **Church Farm** and the **dovecote.** Descend the steep slope to reach a footbridge and stile, and the path leading to the churchyard. Just inside the churchyard, there is a spring to our right. This spring is called the **Holy Well** and is the reason for the church being built on this spot. Before fonts came into use, the spring was used for baptisms. It was also responsible for the development of **Garway village**, and was in use until about 1950. Although the spring had flowed continuously for centuries, it now rises at an outlet slightly higher up the churchyard, though it still flows down the hill to the location of the two fish ponds created in the 12th century.

Herefordshire

Looking towards the church and adjacent Church House.

2 The Manor of Garway was owned from the 12th to the 16th centuries by the Knights Templars and the Knights Hospitallers. The church of **St Michael** was founded between 1165 and 1168. The square 13th century tower was once entirely separate and had been used as a refuge from invading marauders from Wales. The interior contains wonderful 16th-17th century pews, a Norman decorated chancel archway, and a carving of a 'green man' on the left side of the arch. The church was one of only six built by the Templars in England. The original church on this site had a round nave and a square chancel (typical shape of Knights Templars' churches, and a copy of the Holy Sepulchre in Jerusalem). On the outside walls are some mysterious scratched shapes including crosses, and to the right of the church can be seen the remnants of the circular nave, together with the link between the formerly isolated tower and the present day church. Passing to the left side of the church along the narrow gap between the church and the church farm building, reach the door – a visit inside is well worthwhile.

Walk on through the churchyard to the metal gate and along the church drive to the narrow road. Turn left, soon passing the driveway to **Church Farm** and **Church House** - and the **dovecote** which dates from 1326 and contains spaces for 666 birds. Descend along the narrow lane between banks often rich in flowers, snowdrops in spring followed by summer flowers later. Pass a footpath going left, back up to **Church Farm**, and cross over the small stream flowing down from the **Holy Well.** After a further 100 yards, the lane divides and we fork left. Having just descended, we now start to climb, between high banks at first and soon emerging into open country with stunning views all around. Pass between the barns and buildings of **Garway Court**. We continue to climb gently, then level off, and soon begin to descend again.

3 About 300 yards beyond **Garway Court**, a footpath goes right downhill towards Skenfrith, but we turn left through a metal gate and walk uphill along the right margin of a large field. Go over a stile and pass to the right of the house we saw earlier. Reach the road and walk along here to return to the **common** and our starting point.

Places of interest nearby

Skenfrith is 2½ miles south of Garway and has a 13th-century ruined castle, a 13th-century church, a picnic place by the river, and a very smart pub, the Bell.

The little village of **Kilpeck** is 9½ miles to the north of Garway and is home to the famed church of St Mary and St David, with its outstanding collection of stone carvings.

4 **Ledbury**

The Talbot Hotel

Walking **from the centre** of the delightful historic market town of Ledbury takes us past the church, into the Coneygree Wood and over the hill to the tiny village of Eastnor, with its beautiful early 19th-century castle. The return is over the same hill and round the edge of the woods to give wide views over Ledbury as we descend back into the town.

THE PUB The black and white **Talbot Hotel** on New Street has been an inn since 1596. The oak panelled dining room was the scene of a clash in 1645 between Parliamentarians and Royalists, and there is still a bullet in the wall of the

Distance – 4½ miles.

OS Explorer 190 Malvern Hills; **Landranger** 149 Hereford and Leominster with the Eastnor area on Landranger 150 Worcester and The Malverns. GR 711377.

Starting point The Market House in Church Lane in the centre of Ledbury.

How to get there Ledbury is reached via the A449 from Great Malvern and Ross-on-Wye, the A438 from Hereford, or junction 2 of the M50 and the A417. Park in the town centre pay and display car park, or on-street nearby.

restaurant. A barmaid was allegedly shot in this scuffle and her ghost occasionally appears. The fine carving in the restaurant is original, and is the work of A. Noble, a royal carpenter. The initials 'AN' can be seen on one wall, as well as several foxes, his own personal symbol. Bar and restaurant food is available every day, with a wide menu and several fish specials.
☎ *01531 632963*

1 From the 17th-century **Market House** standing on the sixteen oak pillars, walk along the much photographed **Church Lane**. The path leads round the back of the church, and its separate spire, and along the narrow lane to reach the main road. Turn left here and pass **Masefield House**, named after a descendant of the famous poet. Once past the houses cross over to the narrow footpath heading up into **Coneygree Wood**. Climb slightly and pass through a gateway, though not much of the gate remains. When the path divides take the left fork (the right fork is the route of our return near the end of the walk).

Climb steadily, up to a broad horizontal track and cross this to keep straight ahead. Reach a T-junction with a stony track and

Herefordshire

[1] turn left here for about 30 yards. Then turn right along a narrow path and continue climbing. Go on beyond a small wooden gate and bend slightly left, with trees to the left and an open field to the right. Stay close to the field margin as it bends to the right, and then, when it bends again, go left to leave this field, and pass through a few trees and an old gate. At the crosspaths take the track straight ahead, descending slightly to reach an open field. Enjoy the clear view to the embankments of the old camp on the **Herefordshire Beacon** (generally known locally as the **British Camp**).

[2] At the end of the field there is a stile and then a patch of trees as we climb slightly to be joined by a track coming in from the right. Continue to the top of the hill, after which a slight descent

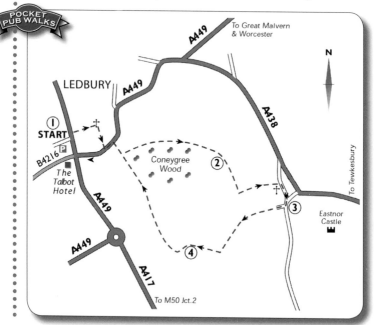

Looking down the main street of the town.

and a bend to the left take us through to a metal gate. Cross the middle of an open field to a gate and a short track, after which we turn left into an open field, where wonderful views of the **Malvern Hills** open up, with **Eastnor Castle, its obelisk** and **Eastnor church** all being prominent. The line of a farm track is our route down the hill and, when the track bends right, keep straight ahead along the footpath, with the hedge, a large house and the church to the right. At the road turn right to the church (well worth a visit), and then reach the village school and the small green, with its water fountain: 'If any man thirst let him come unto me and drink'.

3 The road continues to the village cricket pitch and the castle, but we fork right up the driveway to **Eastnor Pottery**. Pass the pottery and the magnificently restored estate management buildings used as a Range Rover garage. Climb the stony track and, at an open field, look for the small gate where we turn right. Head diagonally up to the far left corner of the field, and go through the metal gate to the right of the buildings. Before

the next gate, turn right along a narrow footpath, with woods to our right. Reach another gate and, once through here, head to the far right corner in the bottom of the field. Here, at two small wooden gates and a footbridge, we enter the woods. Follow the clear path as far as a wooden barrier at the edge of the trees, with a Forestry Commission and **Coneygree Wood** notice.

4 Just before this, turn right along the track, which climbs up into the woods. When it levels off slightly at a crosspaths, the main track keeps straight ahead, and rising, but we turn left here. Follow this path leading through to an old avenue of beech trees, and soon views over **Ledbury** begin to open up down to the left. After a slight rise the footpath divides and we take the left fork, keeping nearer the edge of the woods. A large grassy field slopes down to the town, and this is part of the former estate of **Ledbury Park**. The views across Herefordshire include **Marcle Ridge** with its prominent mast, and the **Welsh hills** beyond. Walk along the edge of the woods and reach the remnant of an old stone wall. The path broadens out and is floored by stone in places (some of which contains fossils). Stay close to the stone wall on the left, and leave the broad track to take a narrow path that goes off to the left by the wall. Quite sunken, this path leads us down to join a path to the right, which was the route of our outward journey. But we keep straight ahead down a few small steps, to reach the road and turn left back into **Ledbury** to the start of the walk.

Places of interest nearby

Eastnor Castle, with the castle and gardens to explore. ☎ 01531 633160

Great Malvern with its springs and wells, theatre and fine Victorian buildings and railway station. *Tourist information centre*, ☎ 01684 892298

5 **Woolhope**

The Crown Inn

This area is known to geologists for the Woolhope Dome where upfolded rocks have been worn away to expose older underlying limestones and shales. Woolhope is set in a conservation area, with several wonderful walks in countryside where wild daffodils and bluebells abound in springtime. Located midway between Ross and Hereford in a very rural part of the county, the village only received mains electricity in 1959. Local stone can be seen in garden walls and also in the pub and St George's church, which are situated close together in the centre of the community. Our walk follows a circular route from the church into the lovely fields and lanes to the south of the village.

Herefordshire

> **Distance** – 3 miles.
>
> **OS Explorer** 189 Hereford and Ross-on-Wye; Landranger 149 Hereford and Leominster. GR 612357.
>
> **Starting point** The parking area by Woolhope's village hall.

How to get there Take the B4224 between Hereford and Ross, and proceed on minor roads via Fownhope or Mordiford; or turn off the A449 Ledbury to Ross road at Much Marcle. Parking is available at the village hall or patrons may leave their cars at the pub (with permission) while they walk.

THE PUB The **Crown Inn** is part stone and part rendered brick. The east end of the building is 500 years old, but the modern parts merge successfully. An ancient relic is the mounting block outside the dining room – with an inset stone dated 1520. There is a small beer garden at the front. This free house offers an excellent choice of beers from Smiles and the Wye Valley Brewery, as well as the local Weston's cider and a good wine list. The wide menu of delicious home-cooked food often includes local beef, liver and rabbit. A variety of snacks are also available.

☎ *01432 860468*

[1] Start from the parking area at the village hall, by the football pitch and tennis courts. Either go to the road and turn left to walk into the village, or cross the playing field to walk along the right side of the church. If walking along the road, pass between modern houses and descend to the T-junction. Turn left here, passing the **Crown Inn**, then the **church,** where the alternative path from the parking place reaches the road. The stone built church with its low squat tower is of Norman origin.

At the road junction notice the oak tree on the small green, commemorating the end of the First World War.

The left fork leads to **Checkley** and **Priors Frome**, the right turn leads to **Sollers Hope**, and ahead to **Putley** and **Ledbury**. Keep straight ahead to pass the fine stone house on the right and the large stone and brick barns. Just beyond the end of the village, go right, over a stile and along the right margin of the field. Pass the stile at the end of the field and continue straight ahead towards the left hand end of the hedge, where there is a stile (but no need for it), as we walk on alongside the hedge on our right. After a further 60 yards veer left and descend to the

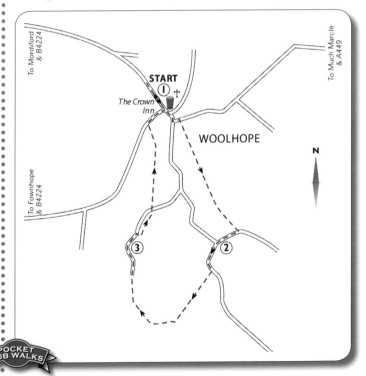

St George's church in Woolhope, seen from its gate.

bottom corner of the field. Go over the stile and immediately turn right over another stile and then left along the edge of the orchard. Follow the hedge as it bends right alongside a stream, to reach a stiled footbridge. Cross the stream here and head across the middle of the next field, aiming towards the mast on **Marcle Ridge**. Reach a stile and the narrow road, where we turn right.

2 When the road divides, fork left to pass the house seen earlier – **Croose Farm**. When this narrow road has an S bend, just past the iron fence on the right, leave the road, going over the stile and across the middle of the field. Aim just to the right of the corner of a fence surrounding a small plantation. Notice the small **Tack Wood** on the hilltop to the left, as we reach a marker post and turn right alongside the line of trees following the ditch. After 50 yards cross the ditch on a plank footbridge

and turn right as far as the hedge where a left turn will lead to a stiled footbridge. Cross over this footbridge and keep ahead alongside the hedge on the right for about 30 yards. Turn right over the stile and cross the middle of the field, heading towards a house visible in the far corner. Go over the stile and along a green lane between hedges, passing **Alford's Mill Cottage** on the right, and then **Alford's Mill Farm**.

3 Where the track, now surfaced, bends left, our path goes straight ahead through an old iron gate and into the field. Stay by the hedge on the right, until it turns right, and then keep straight ahead across the middle of the large field. Reach a stile and a narrow road, and cross straight over to another stile and into a small field. Go over the stiled footbridge and continue across a narrow field to a stile and then the path divides. Take the left fork alongside the hedge, and at the end of this field go on through the gap, still following the hedge. When the hedge turns left, keep ahead to come alongside another hedge and fence on the right. This leads to a stile and we continue up the slope towards large oak trees just to the left of the houses. Reach a road and turn right past **Fairlea**, to walk back into the village. At the road junction turn left to return to the village hall or a few yards ahead to the **Crown**.

Places of interest nearby

Much Marcle, 4 miles from Woolhope, is the home of **Weston's** cider, which has a very informative visitor centre (☎ 01531 660108) with free cider tasting and a children's play area. Also in Much Marcle is the remarkable old house, **Hellens** (☎ 01531 660504), with many historical relics, including a haunted bedroom prepared for Bloody Mary.

The Lichfield Vaults

Hereford, **in the centre of the county**, is both market town and cathedral city and every third year takes its turn at hosting the wonderful music of the Three Choirs Festival. Many ancient buildings, 17th-century and earlier, still survive near the cathedral and High Town. Our walk around the central parts of the city takes in much that is old as well as the new, and also includes a pleasant stroll alongside the River Wye.

THE PUB The centrally placed **Lichfield Vaults** pub is part of the row of old houses along Church Street. The building dates from the 15th century and is reputed to have an underground link with the cathedral. A friendly welcome is accompanied by a large lunchtime menu, ranging from tasty baguettes to full scale meals. Marston's Pedigree and Wells Bombardier are popular beers, and there are two different guest ales each week. The local Bulmers cider is also popular.
☎ 01432 267994

[1] Walk from the **Maylord Orchards car park** and shopping centre into **High Town**, with the timber-framed **Old House** at the east end of High Town. Built in 1621, possibly as the home and shop of a Master Butcher, it was originally part of a row of buildings demolished in the 1830s. The **Old House Museum** opens all year from Tuesday to Saturday, and on Sundays and Bank Holiday Mondays in summer. From the Old House walk along **St Peter's Street** to pass the red sandstone **St Peter's church** with its graceful spire. In the middle of the road is the **war memorial** and in front of the pillared **Shire Hall** building is the

Distance – 2½ miles.

OS Explorer 189 Hereford and Ross-on-Wye; **Landranger** 149 Hereford and Leominster. GR 514400. A detailed town map can be obtained from the Tourist Information Centre (☎ 01432 268430).

Starting point The Maylord Orchards car park.

How to get there Hereford is reached on the A49, the A438 and the A4103. The large Maylord Orchards car park is easily found by following 'Town Centre' signs, but there are several other car parks in the vicinity.

Herefordshire

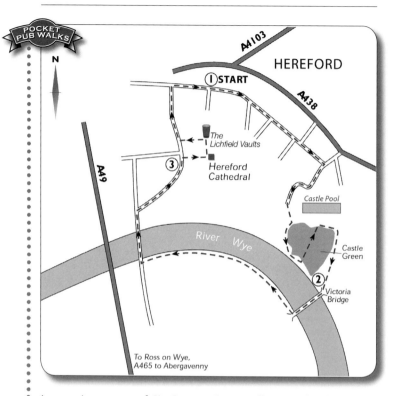

impressive statue of Sir George Cornewall Lewis, local MP and described as a wise and honest statesman. Move on to **St Owen's Street**, passing the **Town Hall** on the right, and then turn right onto **St Ethelbert Street**. At the **Castle House** turn right, and just past **St Ethelbert's Hospital** (dates from the 13th century) take the left turn along the footpath signed to the **Castle Green** and the **River Wye**. Before doing so, walk along the street a few more yards, passing various sections of the **Hereford Cathedral School** to reach number **29 Castle Street**, which was the 14th-century **Hall of Vicars Choral**. Next door is the **Headmaster's house**.

The rear of the hospital can be seen as we pass the long rectangular pond on the left (part of the original moat). Make a circuit of the green, site of an 11th-century castle and now a grassy lawn, with a statue and a bowling green. But do cross the grass to walk to the **Nelson Memorial** of 1809.

2 Beyond the statue in the far left corner of the green are steps down to a narrow road and the **Victoria Suspension Bridge**, constructed in 1898. Cross over the bridge and turn right along the riverside path – to pass a plaque on a large stone to the left of the path to tell us that this is the **Bishop's Meadow**. The riverside walk gives delightful views of the cathedral and then the **Bishop's Palace**, with its riverside gardens and fine cedar tree, as we come to the small statue of the dog. The plaque tells us that near this spot in 1898 occurred the incident depicted in Variation No 11 of Sir Edward Elgar's *Enigma Variations*. Dan the bulldog fell into the river here whilst on a walk with his owner, Dr George Robertson Sinclair, organist at the cathedral, and Sir Edward.

Walk up onto the six-arched bridge, which dates from 1490 though it was damaged in the Civil War and widened in 1826. Turn right to cross the river. Just beyond **Left Bank Village**, a large modern development, take the first turn to the right, to wind through to the cathedral. On the large stone wall to the right of this narrow road is a memorial plaque to Nell Gwynne.

3 Reach the entrance to the **Bishop's Palace** on the right, and another plaque to tell us about the late 12th-century hall, one of the oldest in Britain. Begin to walk up **Broad Street**, but then turn right towards the main (north) door of the cathedral. A visit to the cathedral (founded in the 7th century) is a must, especially as there is the wonderful collection of 1,500 rare books in the **Chained Library** as well as the astonishing 13th-century **Mappa Mundi**.

To the left opposite the main door is the town centre, reached via the pedestrianised **Church Street**. Along here is the **Lichfield**

Herefordshire

The old bridge of 1490.

Vaults, a recommended lunch spot. A few yards beyond 'The Lich' is the **Grapes Tavern**, another of the city's ancient inns, dating from the early 17th century. A plaque on the wall tells of the 'London Letter', which was delivered weekly by stagecoach.

From the cathedral, to complete the circuit of the city centre, walk on along **Broad Street**, with the **Library, Museum and Art Gallery** on the left (closed on Mondays but it is worth going into the doorway to look at the splendid relief map of Herefordshire). On the right is the restored catholic church of **St Francis Xavier**, with its Greek Doric columns. The last building on the right is now **Barclays**, formerly the City Arms, the site of the north gate in the Saxon town, and originally a prominent town house of the Duke of Norfolk. Whilst it was the City Arms Hotel, Nelson stayed here on 23rd August 1802. At the end of Broad Street is **All Saints' church** dating from the 13th century, and here we turn right along **High Street**, to pass the **Butter Market** on the left, just before reaching the **Old House**.

Places of interest nearby

Other attractions in Hereford include the **Cider Museum and King Offa Distillery**, telling the history of cider making, (☎ *01432 354207*), the **Waterworks Museum**, with its collection of pumps, engines and boilers (☎ *01432 361147*), and the **Coningsby Medieval Museum and Chapel** housed in 13th-century almshouses (☎ *01432 274049*).

7 Dorstone

The Pandy Inn

From the old village of Dorstone set in the beautiful Golden Valley, this walk crosses farmland and rises to the edge of the open hilltop of Merbach Hill. It then carries on to reach the remarkable Neolithic Arthur's Stone before descending the valley back to Dorstone. An extension to the walk allows you the opportunity to visit the summit of Merbach Hill to enjoy its superb all-round views, to the Malverns as well as into mid-Wales.

THE PUB The **Pandy Inn** has a beer garden looking out onto the small green and a children's play area. This 12th-century free house is the oldest pub in Herefordshire, and thought to have been built in 1185 by Richard de Brito to provide accommodation for his workers, who were constructing the church. It serves

Distance – 4 miles or nearly 6 miles if carrying on to the top of Merbach Hill

OS Explorer 201 Knighton and Presteigne or OL 13 Brecon Beacons: **Landranger** 148 Presteigne and Hay-on-Wye. GR 314416.

Starting point The Pandy Inn.

How to get there Turn off the A465 Hereford to Abergavenny road on either the B4348 or the B4347 towards Peterchurch. Go on beyond Peterchurch along the B4348 to reach Dorstone. Pub parking is available (with permission) for patrons while they walk; alternatively, leave your car near the green or village hall.

excellent home-made food, with a slight Polish influence, and there is a wide menu to suit all tastes. ☎ *01981 550273*

1 An old motte and bailey is located behind the **Pandy Inn**, but we walk in the opposite direction, to the small green and the sun dial – formerly a village cross. Keep straight ahead to go over the little **River Dore** (taking its name from *d'Or*, or the Welsh *dwfr* meaning water) and pass to the left of the church of **St Faith**, with its short squat 13th-century tower.

At the road turn right for a few yards and then left through a kissing gate. Pass the bowling green and fork diagonally left across the field to a footbridge and a stile. Cross a track that follows the line of the Golden Valley railway, built in 1870s. The last trains ran in 1950. Continue ahead across the next field, to reach a stile and a track (**Spoon Lane**). Go up a few steps and keep straight ahead, to reach a farm track. Turn left here to **Llan Farm**, passing through the farmyard. Stay on the stony track as it climbs steadily. When it begins to level off, turn right to the top of the field to a stile and a narrow road.

[2] Turn left here for about 5 yards, then right along the field margin. Reach a stile in the corner of the field, and walk out onto a track where we turn left. After 60 yards turn right over a stile, and go through two fields. Pass a house on the right, and at the narrow road, turn left.

[3] *For the 4 mile walk,* stay on the road when it bends right, and after about 200 yards turn right towards **New Farm**, continuing from point 5.

For the longer walk, when the road turns right, go straight ahead through the gate and continue along the track. When this bends

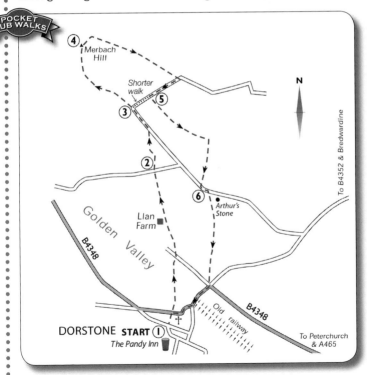

left, keep straight ahead, alongside the remnants of a former hedge. Climb slightly, and then begin to move to the right away from the hedge to go up to the highest point we can see, with a tall box and an aerial as our target. From here, we can walk on through the small wooden gate to reach the triangulation point (318 m, 1,043 ft) at the top of the red sandstone **Merbach Hill**. Turn right here, but first enjoy the wonderful all round views – **Malverns**, **River Wye**, **Clee Hill**, **Hay Bluff**.

4 Notice the evidence of old quarrying around the triangulation point. As we move on (south-east) close to the left edge of the uneven ground, follow a narrow path, which leads through bracken. Do not go downhill and off to the left just yet. The path winds through rough vegetation of bracken and brambles and as we begin to descend, the number of small trees increases. Reach a green bridleway between hedges and keep straight ahead, approaching an old skeletal corrugated iron barn. Join a narrow road on a right-angled bend, where we turn right and climb slightly. At the farm drive to **New Farm**, turn left.

5 Walk along the farm drive. Just beyond the farmhouse, go right through a gate and immediately left to continue straight ahead. Pass through gates and two fields, until reaching a small clump of fir trees. Here we turn right and head across the field to a metal gate. Continue along the left side of the next field, to another gate and a narrow road. Turn left here and walk as far as **Arthur's Stone** – a multi-chambered tomb of the Neolithic period from between 3700 and 2700 BC, with a massive capstone 20 ft in length. Flint tools and pottery have been found around here.

6 From **Arthur's Stone** go over the new stile and across the field to a stile and onto the line of a farm track, which leads us downhill. A small pond is down to our left, as we descend along the track to a stile by a gate. Follow the line of this track through the fields down to the first houses of **Dorstone** and the road. At the four-way junction, keep straight ahead along the B4348. On reaching

with a large stone slab. Pass through another field to a stile and then into the woods. Descend slightly to reach a stile, and then continue downhill along the left side of the field, to reach a track and continue descending. Reach a very trendy stile, with two rungs that lift up to enable small people to cross with ease. Walk on down the drive, passing to the left of the recently modernised **Cheyney Court**, and at the road

St Mary's church.

(sign to '**Cheyney Park**' and '**Chapel**') turn right. Reach a T-junction and turn left, to walk on past the old mill, also recently modernised. Cross over the river bridge and turn right through the kissing gate. Follow the right margin of the field, close to the river. At the end of this field is the old **Vicarage** over to the left, and we turn left to walk back into the churchyard and our starting point.

Places of interest nearby

The **Hop Pocket Farm Shop** (which also sells craft products) and café are along the B4214 to the south.

Castle Frome, 2 miles south of Bishops Frome, has a church with a remarkable decorated font.

9 Sutton Saint Nicholas

The Golden Cross

The parishes of St Michael and St Nicholas merged into one village, which explains the survival of two churches. St Michael's church is of Norman origin with the east window and font dating from those times, whilst St Nicholas' church dates from the 12th century. This interesting walk leaves the village to walk across farmland and riverside meadows rich in wildlife. It then heads towards Marden and through orchards on the climb up to the Iron Age fort on Sutton Walls, which was built on the ridge overlooking the River Lugg and covers 30 acres. Much quarrying damaged the land surface, but excavations have revealed use over a long period including 1st and 2nd centuries AD. Relics can be seen in Hereford museum.

THE PUB The **Golden Cross** has been a pub for nearly 200 years, and was originally a small inn and an adjoining cottage. Recently a major refurbishment and extension have produced the smart, modern and very attractive pub and restaurant we see today. The comfortable lounge bar in this free house contains a pool table, and upstairs is the spacious restaurant. There is also a garden for eating outside on hot summer days. The pub stands at the village crossroads and serves local people as well as motorised customers – and walkers – from further afield. Local produce appears on the menu, including Herefordshire beef and local game in season.

☎ 01432 880274

1 From the crossroads by the pub, follow the sign towards **Marden**, and after about 150 yards take the first turning to the left, with the old post office (now a private residence) on the right. After 100 yards turn right over a small (broken down) stile and cross a small field to a stiled footbridge and then along the right margin of the next field. Reach a stile in the right corner of the field, and proceed along the narrow grassy track to another stile to

Distance – 5 miles or 6 miles if you decide to walk around the hill fort.

OS Explorer 202 Leominster and Bromyard; **Landranger** 149 Hereford and Leominster. GR 533455.

Starting point The Golden Cross in Sutton St Nicholas.

How to get there From the A465/A4103 junction ½ mile north of Hereford, head northwards along a minor road signed to Bodenham and Sutton St Nicholas. Patrons may park at the pub (with permission) while they walk. Alternatively, park in the nearby streets or close to the church of St Nicholas.

pass between houses. Reach a narrow lane and continue over the stile and straight ahead across the next field. To the right is the small church of **St Michael**, but our way ahead is the stile about 60–70 yards to the left of the church. Keep straight ahead across the middle of the next field, close to the telegraph pole, and then across another field to reach a stile – just to the left of **Freens Court Farm**, which still has remains of an old moat. Our path goes on from the stile, slightly left of straight ahead to a stiled footbridge. Once across the ditch, bend right to a stile and across a huge field, aiming to the right of the buildings.

[2] Reach the road and just on the left is the old stone bridge over the **River Lugg**, and beyond that the railway. Move 20 yards to the right along the road and then go on over the stile in the hedge. Stay close to the river at first, but then move slightly to the right to reach a stile and keep ahead across the next two

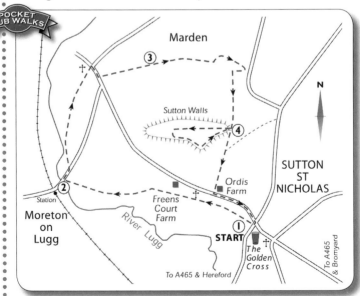

Moreton bridge, over the River Lugg.

fields, passing through gates. Cross the cattle bridge over a small stream and head towards the white house in the far right corner of the next field. Large black and white houses and barns are slightly to the left of this house. Further to the left is **Marden church**, situated along the river bank. Here was the site of the burial of King Ethelbert in AD 793 after he had been killed by King Offa, though later his body was moved to Hereford Cathedral. Cross a stile, a small field and another stile to reach the road. Directly opposite is a **war memorial**. Turn right along the road, and after about 40 yards go left over a stile and along the track between open fields. Keep straight ahead across two fields to reach a hedge with a crosspaths.

[3] Keep straight ahead here, passing to the right of a lone oak tree and an old shed, to a stile in the hedge. Go on over this to walk alongside the hedge on the left, with a huge orchard (one of the largest in the county) stretching away to the right. Stay close to the hedge as it bends left, and then right and, as it approaches houses bend right again, still following the hedge to the left. On reaching a large surfaced area, with the small stone **Cider House**

ahead, turn right on the surfaced track to pass the large barn. After 100 yards the stony track bends left, and we follow this between orchards. When this stony drive turns right, we keep straight ahead along the grassy track, with a windbreak line of hornbeam on our left. After about 70 yards, as we are beginning to climb, move slightly left, to go through the gate and walk along the right margin of the field. Go on up the hill, passing the eastern end of **Sutton Walls**.

4 *At this point a diversion is possible.* A few yards into the woods is the clear path that makes a circuit of the fort. From here a short climb reaches the top of the hill fort and a large cropped field. Beyond the field is a grassy and scrub area, and the site of former quarrying. Once beyond this, turn left at the crosspaths and after a few yards turn left again, to follow the path that runs along the south side of the hill fort and will lead back to our point of diversion.

Once back on our original path, begin to descend the hill. At the bottom, pass through a gate and soon we are joined by a track coming in from the left (**Franklands Gate**). Follow this broad green track between hedges, as it leads us back to the road to pass **The Granary** and **Ordis Farm** on our left. At the road turn left to walk back to the crossroads by the **Golden Cross**.

Places of interest nearby

Hereford has much to interest visitors, notably the cathedral with the **Mappa Mundi** and the **Chained Library** (see Walk 6).

Queenswood Country Park is 3 miles to the north of Sutton St Nicholas, with a visitor centre and signed walks around the woods
☎ *01568 798320*

10 Weobley

The Red Lion Hotel

Weobley is considered by many to be the finest of Herefordshire's black and white villages. The walk takes us along the main street passing between many half-timbered buildings, some of which date from the 14th to 16th centuries. We continue by strolling through the old castle site, across the park and into the beautiful rural countryside that surrounds the village. The route starts and ends by the church of St Peter and St Paul, which is well worth a visit. Parts date back to the early 13th century when it was built by Hugh de Lacy, the Lord of the Manor – on the site of an earlier wooden building. The tower was added in the 14th century and is not quite in line with the nave. Amongst the other interesting features are memorials to the Birch family, who lived in Garnstone House – which was rebuilt by Nash in 1807, but demolished in 1959.

Distance – 4½ miles.

OS Explorer 202 Leominster and Bromyard; **Landranger** 149 Hereford and Leominster. GR 401517.

Starting point The car park at the northern end of Weobley village.

How to get there *Take the A4112, which runs between the A44 south-west of Leominster and the A438 north-east of Hay-on-Wye. Weobley is ½ mile off this road along the B4230, and a signposted car park is at the northern end of the village not far from the church.*

John Birch was a prominent Parliamentarian, and was probably responsible for rebuilding the church spire in 1675 (at 185 ft, the highest in the county).

THE PUB The **Red Lion Hotel**, passed at the beginning and end of the walk, is one of Weobley's finest black and white buildings, and dates from the 14th century. This privately owned pub, restaurant and hotel is open all day from 12 noon and its bar offers pool, darts and TV. The spacious and comfortable restaurant has a wide menu offering much local produce. Traditional Sunday lunch is one noted speciality, and booking is advisable for this.
☎ *01544 318220*

1 Turn left out of the car park – although it is worth making a short detour to visit the church either now or at the end of the walk. Follow the road into the village. Pass the **Red Lion Hotel** on the left, and then bend right to walk along **Broad Street**, with its amazing collection of old black and white buildings. Near the end is the small green, the former location of the cattle market

– which was noted for Hereford cattle. There was a market hall here until it was demolished in the mid 19th century.

Take the left fork alongside the green, and at the T-junction walk straight ahead along a short drive to the entrance to **Garnstone Park**, where there is an information board for **Weobley Castle**. The Norman castle of which only the earthworks remain, was originally built by the de Lacys (Laceys). Walk beneath the line of large old oak trees, crossing the moat and the earthworks of the ancient castle, to reach a kissing gate, beyond which is the open parkland. Take the middle of the three options, heading slightly right. Cross the large field to a wooden kissing gate by

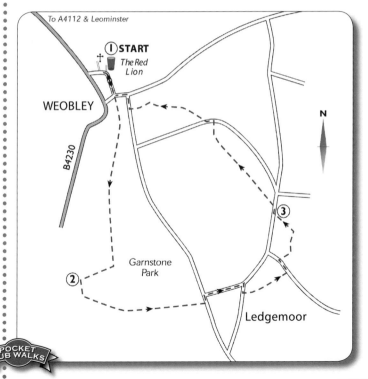

Herefordshire

a metal gate, with the green 'Circular Walk' sign. Climbing gently, keep straight ahead, and just before reaching a small wood, go through a kissing gate. Turn right before the gate into the woods, and pass to the right of the house and then the large garden wall.

The main street of Weobley, looking towards the church.

2 At the end of this wall turn left through a wooden kissing gate, and take the path diagonally left across to the far corner of the large field. Go on over the stile, along a track lined by large oak trees. Across to the left can be seen the ruins of **Garnstone House** and a small pond. Continue along the track to walk through to a narrow road. Turn left here for 20 yards and then turn right along the road signed to **Ledgemoor**, and **Marshpools Inn**. Turn at the first road to the right, still signed 'Circular Walk', and after 30 yards go left along the footpath close to the right margin of the field. This leads through to a gate and a narrow road opposite a house – and we turn left. After 100 yards turn right along a narrow road, which deteriorates to a stony drive. When we reach a garden gate, turn right along the narrow path between houses. Go over the stile

and footbridge and turn left along the field margin for a few yards, and then go left over the stile in the hedge. Turn right here and head diagonally across the field, aiming just to the left of the lone house. At the stile, cross the road to another stile where there are two paths.

3 Follow the green 'Circular Walk' sign, and take the right fork, diagonally across the field, over a stile and slightly left across the next field to a gap in the hedge. Continue straight on across the fields to reach a broad grassy path – and a road. Cross to the stile, and head diagonally left across the field, to a stile, and diagonally right to a gap in the hedge. Cross one more field to a stile – and onto a narrow path. Just before reaching a gate, stile and houses, turn right along a grassy path between hedges. Reach a surfaced path and turn left, and then the path bends right, passing between bungalows. Walk on round to a narrow path between fence, hedge and houses, and this leads through to a road. Turn right here, passing between more of the remarkable houses of **Weobley**, to reach the old 16th-century buildings, the former **Grammar School** and the **Throne House**. King Charles is reputed to have stayed in the latter (hence the name) on the 5th September 1645, after the Battle of Naseby. At the T-junction turn left, passing the 17th-century **Unicorn** to return to **Broad Street** and the end of the walk.

Places of interest nearby

Weobley Museum of Local History is in Back Lane, on the site of the former court and police station. ☎ 01544 319212.

Pembridge, a few miles to the north is another of Herefordshire's black and white villages, whilst **Hay-on-Wye**, to the south-west, is famed for its second-hand bookshops.

11 **Kington**

The Swan Hotel

The old market town of Kington is located on Offa's Dyke footpath, and at the end of the Mortimer Trail, which extends 30 miles to Ludlow. Our walk takes us along the attractive Arrow Valley and then up onto Hergest Ridge, famed for its bracing air and fine views. Following the route of Offa's Dyke long distance footpath, we return to town alongside the edge of Hergest Croft Gardens, which attract many visitors at all seasons. The church of St Mary the Virgin, passed at the end of the walk, has a Norman font and the tower dates from 12th century. Other parts of the church are from 12th and 13th centuries. The spire is 18th-century and has been recently restored. Well-preserved alabaster tombs are of Thomas Vaughan and his wife Ellen who lived at Hergest Court – which is now mostly decayed although part still survives as a farmhouse. Thomas was slain at Banbury in 1469 and it is reputed that his wife, known as Ellen the Terrible, shot an arrow through the heart of his murderer.

THE PUB The **Swan Hotel** is comfortable and welcoming, with a restaurant area and a Walkers' Bar. Meals are home-cooked using local produce and the wide menu will suit all tastes. One of the specials on my last visit was wild mushroom risotto to coincide with the Herefordshire Mushroom week. The real ales offered are from the local breweries, Spinning Dog and Wood's. Overnight accommodation is also available.
☎ 01544 230510

1 From the **Swan** walk down **Church Street** towards the town centre. At the T-junction turn right along **Mill Street**, passing the **Burton Hotel** on the left and the **Coach House** and **Market Hall** on the right. One of the town's information plaques tells us that the Market Hall was built in 1885, as was the adjacent

> **Distance** – 3 miles, plus extra in Hergest Croft Gardens perhaps.
>
> **OS Explorer** 201 Knighton and Presteigne; **Landranger** 148 Presteigne and Hay-on-Wye. GR 295567.
>
> **Starting point** The Swan Hotel, Church Street, Kington.

How to get there Kington lies to the south of the A44 Leominster to Rhayader road. Turn into the town centre and continue to Church Street. Patrons may leave their cars at the Swan (with permission) while they walk. Alternatively, park in the Square adjacent to the pub.

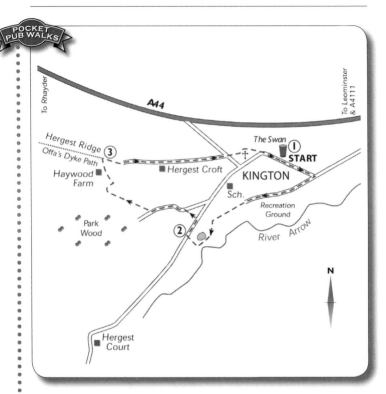

POCKET PUB WALKS

To Rhayder

A44

To Leominster & A4111

Hergest Ridge ③
Offa's Dyke Path

The Swan ①
START

Haywood Farm

Hergest Croft

KINGTON

Sch.

Recreation Ground

Park Wood

②

River Arrow

N

Hergest Court

Dutch gabled building on the site of the King's Head Inn. Pass the **Tourist Information Centre** (telephone: 01544 230778) and pay and display car park on the left, before reaching the entrance gates to the **Recreation Ground**. The **Memorial Gates** were erected in honour of the men who served in the Great War.

Walk along the path inside the 'Rec', straight through to the far end. Leave via the large gate to the right of the pavilion and keep ahead through the fields – with the **River Arrow** 30 or 40 yards to the left. When a pond can be seen on the right, a path passes to the right of this and out to the road, but it is better to stay left of the pond, walking alongside the river as far as the footbridge. Do not cross the river, but turn right at the footbridge to a small wooden gate, which leads to a path. Cross a stone slab footbridge, and pass on the left side of a stone barn and then a stone house (**Hergest Mill**). Walk out through the garden to reach the narrow road and turn right.

2 About 100 yards along this road go left up a few steps to a stile and walk up the right margin of the field. When the hedge begins to bend to the left, go right, over a stile and onto the narrow lane. Turn left and follow this between banks and hedges, passing **Nant y Felin** and climbing steadily. Parkland of the **Hergest Croft Gardens** can be seen to our right. At a cattle grid the track divides, by the **Haywood Common** signpost. The left fork is to **Park Wood**, but we fork right, following the bridleway sign. Still climbing, reach a crosspaths at post numbered **13**, and to the

The gardens of Hergest Croft.

Herefordshire

right is an entrance point to the parkland. Keep straight ahead, with the grassy bank on our left, sloping down to the valley with woods to the other side. Our track bends right and then left to pass **Haywood farmhouse**. Follow the track through a large metal gate and the farmyard to continue the climb.

[3] Reach the narrow surfaced road, which goes left onto **Hergest Ridge**, but we turn right. Parking spaces are available here for anyone wishing to walk along the Ridge. Begin to descend, with views into **Hergest Croft Gardens** to the right – the interesting assortment of trees and shrubs might whet your appetite for a visit. Emerge from the woods so that views open up to the left. Continue to descend more steeply, passing the turreted house to the left, and soon reach the major road. Cross straight over here and walk up to the **church of St Mary the Virgin**, perched on top of the hill near the site of the former castle. Notice the remnants of a medieval preaching cross outside the main door of the church and close to the external tower steps. Walk on through the 18th-century lychgate and out to the road. Notice on the left the old tower on **Castle Hill** with the 'Kington Past' information plaque no 6. Continue along the main road, back to the starting point.

Places of interest nearby

Hergest Croft Gardens, passed on the walk, are open every afternoon from 1st April to 31st October. The 50 acres of garden include open parkland and woodland as well as flower borders, kitchen garden, a wide range of trees and a special area of azaleas.
☎ 01544 230160

The **Small Breeds Farm and Owl Centre** is at Kingswood, 2 miles south of Kington along the A4111.
☎ 01544 2231109; www.owlcentre.com

12 **Bromyard Downs**

The Royal Oak

Bromyard Downs extend over 262 acres, and these open fields have been used to graze stock for many years. There are still 89 properties around the Downs with grazing rights attached to them, though very few take advantage of these rights. Sheep do graze on the common but much of the grass has to be cut for hay in the summer to prevent bracken and bushes taking over. In the past, when drovers were passing through on their way to markets, they used the fields near Warren Wood for their cattle and had to pay a halfpenny per cow for an overnight stop. Parts of the Downs were ploughed for a few years during the Second World War in order to grow food but much has not been cultivated for centuries, and is rich in flowers and grasses as a result. There were quarries here at one time, providing building stone for houses in the area. The rock is from the geological period called the Old Red Sandstone, dating from nearly 400 million years ago. This shortish walk takes us to the top of the Downs at a height of 780 ft with stunning all round views, and then circles round farmland and through the woods, before recrossing the Downs back to the starting point.

THE PUB The old oak-beamed **Royal Oak** inn, just north of the parking area on Bromyard Downs, dates from the 17th century and began life as a cider house. A few apple trees still remain from the orchards. The inn provided space for administration, storage and relaxation for the users of the nearby rifle range in former times. Food is served every lunchtime, and the Sunday carvery is very popular – booking is advisable for this. A wide selection is available on the daily menu, including steak and kidney pie and lasagne, both home-made. Walkers are encouraged, and all visitors will receive a friendly welcome. There is a playground for children and ample outdoor space.
☎ *01885 482585*

Distance – nearly 3 miles.

OS Explorer 202 Leominster and Bromyard; **Landranger** 149 Hereford and Leominster. GR 671558.

Starting point The parking and picnic place on the edge of the common, to the south of the Royal Oak inn.

How to get there About 2 miles east of Bromyard along the A44 Worcester to Bromyard road, turn along the narrow unfenced road signed to Bromyard Downs and the Royal Oak. Park at the picnic area on the right.

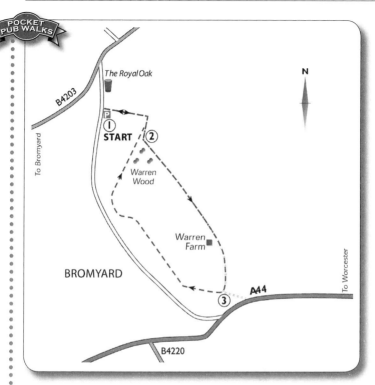

POCKET
PUB WALKS

The Royal Oak

N

B4203

To Bromyard

P

① START ②

Warren
Wood

Warren
Farm

BROMYARD

To Worcester

A44

③

B4220

1 From the parking place walk east, over the small footbridge, and head straight up the hill, with a small house a few yards to the left. Go on up the grassy downland, crossing the location of the rifle range, and then on up to the level grassy track running to left and right. This was the old race track, which was laid out at the beginning of the 19th century, possibly by ex soldiers returning home from the Napoleonic wars, at a time with few jobs and an economic slump. Racing ended on the course in 1904. Go on beyond here, up to the top edge of the common, and turn right. Walk along to **Shepherd's Cottage**.

Herefordshire

Bromyard Downs.

2 Go through the small gate near the large gate to pass to the left of the house, admiring an unusual assortment of interesting objets d'art. Then go on through another gate, to the narrow path between a hedge on the left and a barbed wire fence and open field on the right. At the end of this path, pass through a new gate, with a small pond to the right. Keep ahead along the field margin, with the hedge to the right. Continue through or over a large metal gate, and go straight ahead along the farm track. Enjoy the wonderful views to the left, looking across at the ridge of hills extending from **Suckley** towards **Abberley**. Pass the barns and then the farmhouse of **Warren Farm**, and note the track that goes off left here, down into the valley and towards the **Brockhampton Estate** – a very good extension walk here if required.

But we keep ahead, to where the farm drive bends left to go down to the road.

3 Turn right here along a field margin, with the hedge on our right – and follow the footpath sign. At the end of this field, go over the stile and turn right, along the grassy path at the top of the Downs. Trees and hedge are to the right and a grassy slope goes down to the left – to the narrow road. Good views open up over **Bromyard** and the hills beyond. Walk along to reach the woodland area, **Warren Wood**. Pass through the kissing gate into the woods, by the NT plaque on a stone pillar. Turn left on the path, staying close to the edge of the woods. Ignore the next kissing gate on the margin of the woods to the left, and continue ahead. The path begins to bend to the right and then climbs slightly to another NT sign by a stile, with a very convenient narrow handle at the top of the pole. Go on over this stile and keep straight ahead by a line of trees on our right, to reach **Shepherd's Cottage** again (point 2). Continue ahead for a few more yards, before turning left to descend across the former race track and down to the picnic parking area on the edge of a clump of trees. The **Royal Oak** is a few yards along the road.

Places of interest nearby

The small and historic town of **Bromyard** is well worth a visit, with a Heritage Centre, several 17th-century black and white houses and an old grammar school dating back to 1394.

Tourist Information Centre, ☎ *01432 260280*

A short distance aong the road towards Worcester is the **Brockhampton Estate** with the idyllic **Lower Brockhampton House** (NT). The chapel remains are from the 12th century and the gatehouse is 15th-century.

☎ *(Lower Brockhampton House): 01885 488099*

13 Leominster

The Bell

Leominster grew as a wool town and retains many old black and white buildings. Outstanding sights are the magnificent priory church of St Peter and St Paul and the adjacent Grange Court, which was the old town hall built in 1633 by the King's carpenter, John Abel. The church began as a nunnery in pre-Norman times and was founded as a Benedictine priory in 1123. It is part Norman but with many more recent changes. Amongst numerous features of interest are three parallel naves, 19th-century stained-glass windows by Charles Kempe, a painting of the Wheel of Life that probably dates from 1275, and the last ducking stool used in England (in 1809). Our walk begins and ends with a gentle perambulation round the centre of this attractive market town but also includes a stretch

Distance – 4½ miles.

OS Explorer 202 Leominster and Bromyard; **Landranger** 149 Hereford and Leominster. GR 496593.

Starting point The free car park off Bridge Street. GR 496593.

How to get there *The A49 and A44 meet at Leominster. At the northern end of the A49 bypass turn into the town, signed as the A44 to Rhayader. Cross the railway and bend left into the main street and the car park is on the left.*

alongside the River Lugg and a climb up to the top of Eaton Hill with views across Leominster and towards the hills of Wales. From Eaton Hill, the route descends to pass a garden centre and the magnificent buildings of Eaton Hall before returning to the town.

THE PUB The **Bell**, a lively, welcoming free house in Etnam Street, reached towards the end of the walk, is open all day. Log fires and beautiful gardens are seasonal attractions. There is a good choice of real ales, including those from the Wye Valley Brewery at Stoke Lacy, south of Bromyard. The menu offers a selection of tasty freshly cooked food, as well as a range of sandwiches.
☎ *01568 612818*

1 Walk from the far end of the car park, most distant from the main road. Turn right along the footpath signed to **Priory Church** and **Grange Court**. Pass (or visit) the **priory church of St Peter and St Paul**. Just before reaching Grange Court notice the large oak tree with the small plaque to inform us that the acorn for this tree came from Verdun during the First World War. Turn left and walk

through the children's playground or on the small playing field alongside, to reach the **Riverside Millennium Green**. Turn right alongside the railway – quite a busy line taking the hourly service from South Wales to Manchester and Liverpool. Pass through a small orchard, then a workshop yard to reach the **White Lion** (the first of several excellent pubs passed in Leominster). Turn immediately left along the narrow path (signed '**Herefordshire Trail**') and use the footbridge to cross the railway line.

2 Take the farm bridge across the **River Lugg**, and turn left down onto the riverside path. Walk between **Brightwell's** (Auctioneer

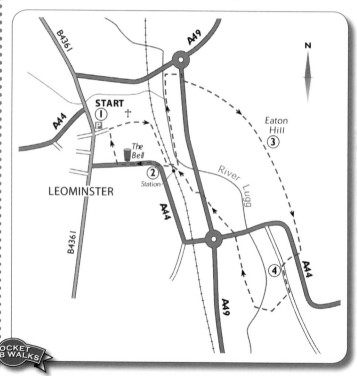

and Valuers) on the right and the river to our left, passing the confluence of the **Lugg** and the **Kenwater**. Go over a stile onto the driveway into Brightwell's and then to the road, where we turn right. At the main A49 road, cross over at the island and turn right. Walk southwards alongside the road for about 70 yards, then turn left through a gate on the long driveway. Walk on past the large modern house, and as the stony track bends right, we begin to climb through small trees and bushes, up towards the mast – with good views across **Leominster** and towards the **Welsh hills**.

Leominster Priory.

3 At the top of the slope we keep ahead, with the large metal gate and the mast to our left. Pass over two stiles to reach an open field and walk along the right margin, by the hedge. About 100 yards before the end of the field, stay close to the hedge and take the narrow path downhill. Reach a stile by a gate and crosspaths, but keep straight ahead, still descending along a grassy track. At the end of the trees, keep straight on to a large wooden five-barred gate. Cross straight over the main A44 road to a stile and a grassy track between fences. Notice the grove of eucalyptus trees. The track leads through to a narrow road, with the **West Eaton Nurseries** to the right.

4 Turn left here and walk along the road for about 200 yards. Turn right along the farm driveway and this leads us through the farmyard of the large farm complex at **Eaton Hall**, part of

Herefordshire

which dates from the 14th century. Cross the river, and turn right along the river bank. Go over a stile and leave the river bank to head diagonally left towards the far right corner of the field. Go on over a stile and along the right margin of the field and then along the left margin of the next field to reach the road (the A44 again). Cross straight over and along the drive close to the house, to reach a metal gate. Go through here and along the left margin of a large field. Just before reaching the pumping station, go through a small gate and up the steps to the road. Cross over to a gate on the other side. Bear slightly right in the small field, following an old embankment to reach a stile near the river bridge crossed earlier (point 2). Bend left away from the river to go over the footbridge across the railway. Pass the **White Lion** again, and walk ahead along **Etnam Street**. We pass the **Chequers** (dates from 1600), and then the **Bell**, both on the right. The **Folk Museum** is on the left – open April to October (telephone: 01568 615186), and opposite is **School Lane**. Turn right here to reach the **Corn Square** by the **Three Horseshoes**. From the end of **School Lane**, turn right to walk along the footpath signed to **Priory Church** and **Grange Court** – and thence to the car park.

Places of interest nearby

The National Trust's **Berrington Hall** is 3 miles to the north – an 18th-century mansion set in a landscape created by Capability Brown
☎ *01568 615721*

Stockton Bury Gardens at Kimbolton, can be found just off the A49 north of Leominster, along the A4112. They consist of a 4-acre garden set in beautiful countryside, with old agricultural buildings and a dovecote.
☎ *01568 613432*

The Bateman Arms

The delightful old village, remarkable church, historic ruins and glorious countryside are all part of this circular walk across the fields around Shobdon – with ever changing views across Herefordshire and into Wales. It is well worth spending some time looking round St John's church. The tower is 13th-century but the remainder is 18th-century, built to the design of Horace Walpole in the style known as Strawberry Hill Gothic. The interior is Wedgwood blue with stucco panelling and gothic furnishings. It's quite a surprise when you go in – a kind of wedding cake rococo! The original Norman church was demolished to make way for this Georgian building, as instructed by Viscount Bateman, who owned Shobdon Court, with some of the arches being re-sited in the parkland about ¼ mile to the north. The Court itself was built in the early 1700s but was largely demolished in 1933.

Herefordshire

Distance – 5 miles.

OS Explorer 203 Ludlow (start and end) and 201 Knighton and Presteigne; **Landranger** 149 Hereford and Leominster. GR 401629.

Starting point Parking area near the church in Shobdon.

How to get there From Mortimer's Cross on the A4110 Hereford to Knighton road, take the B4362 to Shobdon. Before reaching the village, turn right along the narrow road signed to Shobdon church and the Arches to park near the church. Alternatively, patrons may leave their cars at the Bateman Arms (with permission) while they walk – in this case you would carry on into the village along the B4362 and start the walk at point 4.

THE PUB The **Bateman Arms** inn and restaurant dates from 1720s and is a Grade II listed building. A free house, it offers a wide menu of full-scale meals, as well as snacks or sandwiches, in a very relaxed atmosphere. We sampled a hot bacon and cheese salad, and a beef open sandwich with salad – very tasty, and filling too.
☎ *01568 708374*

1. Start from the large parking area near the church and the visitor centre. Follow the sign to the **Arches**, climbing steadily along the avenue of trees, with a small pond on the left and the cricket pitch to the right. Information boards tell us that these arches are all that remains of the Romanesque church built in the 1130s and replaced in 1751. The carvings have unfortunately all suffered from weathering. Some of the sculptors involved here – all part of the Herefordshire School of Romanesque Sculpture – had also worked at Kilpeck, Leominster Priory and elsewhere.

Turn left at the **Arches**, and walk along the top edge of a field, with woodland to the right. After about 30 yards bear right into the woods, to reach a narrow road. Turn left, passing **Uphampton Farm** and **Uphampton House** on the right. Then reach **The Parks** on the left, and large buildings rearing chickens for Sun Valley.

2 Turn right off the road, along a narrow lane signed 'Public Footpath' and 'Circular Walk'. At the end of this lane turn left for a few yards before the gate and fenced area of **Shobdon Field Station**. Walk along the right margin of a large field, with trees to the right. The good views to the left extend to **Hay Bluff**. Just past a few buildings on the right, the 'Circular Walk' is signed over to the right, but we keep ahead along the field margin. In

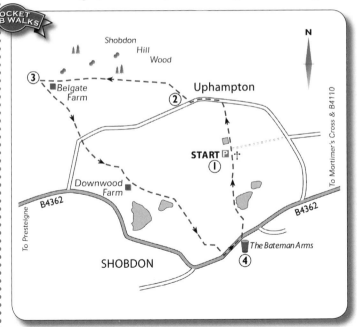

St John's church in Shobdon.

the corner of the field, go through the patch of trees and shrubs to reach a hedge and stile and keep ahead diagonally across the next field, aiming halfway along the hedge. At the far side of the field, go on through a gap and stay close to the hedge on the left side of the next field. This leads us to a gate and we keep straight ahead into the next field, still close to the hedge on our left. Pass the buildings of **Belgate Farm** in a very sheltered location, and once beyond all the buildings turn sharp left.

3 The driveway leads down to a metal gate and beyond here we pass to the right side of all the buildings. As you descend look back at the house and lawn fronted by a stone wall and ha-ha. Walk on down to a narrow road and go straight ahead, through the gate and across the field. Continue to the far left corner of the next field sloping down to a stile. Proceed along the right side of a small field, with **Downwood Farm** to our right. Stay close to the fence on our right, descend a small hill and go right over the stile at the bottom – signed '**Mortimer Trail**' and '**Circular Walk**'. Cross to another stile, beyond which we turn left along

the hedge. After the next stile turn right alongside the fence on our right. Near the end of this field, bend left, to reach another stile, beyond which we head diagonally left across a larger field. Go on over the stile and turn right, along the margin of the field, with a wood to our right. Soon pass a pool to the right, and a chalet park through the trees. Go on over the next stile, onto a golf course. Turn left and follow the margin of the course, bending right but staying close to the hedge. When the hedge turns left, keep straight ahead, and follow the line of trees to the end of the golf course. Go on over the stile and turn left. Pass through two small fields with the hedge to the left, then over another stile and turn right. Cross the field to a stile and then continue along a narrow path between houses and gardens, to reach a driveway leading out to the main road in **Shobdon** village – with a converted chapel on our left. Turn left along the road, and soon pass the old cider press on our right as we walk to the **Bateman Arms**.

4 Stop for refreshment, or walk on a few more yards then turn left along the driveway signed to **Shobdon Court**. Pass a landscaped pool on the right and begin to climb gradually, then a long pool on the left and the walled garden (now no longer used for vegetables). Pass the old Servants' Block on the right – now flats – to reach the remarkable church and our starting point. Now visit the church!

Places of interest nearby

The black and white villages of **Pembridge** and **Eardisland**, 3 miles to the south of Shobdon are well worth a visit.

Croft Castle (National Trust) is 5 miles to the north-east and reached from the B4362.

☎ *01568 780246*

The Lion Hotel

The historic village of Leintwardine has had a long existence. It was an important river crossing of the Clun and Teme, and was a strategic centre very important to the Romans – named Bravinium (or Branogenium). They had a fortress at Buckton and another at Jay Lane, and the Roman road Watling Street West dates from AD 50/60. High Street, the main road through the village, runs along the line of Watling Street extending south to the remains of Wigmore Abbey. About AD 170 a massive rampart was built around the settlement, with a series of ditches enclosing about 10 acres, from the river crossing northwards. All artefacts from the Roman period are now in Ludlow Museum. The large sandstone church of St Mary Magdalene is on the site of a Saxon church. The oldest part of the present church is the blocked up doorway in the west wall of the nave. Beneath this are the much older remnants of the Roman embankment. The tall pillars in the nave are round on the south side, but octagonal on the north side. The famous old clock in the church dates from at least the early 16th century, and is the oldest in the county. The present day village has several old thatched cottages and a few grand houses, as well as some modern developments.

Our circuit is a flat, low and level walk, crossing a watery landscape with three rivers. Ever present and all around us are the wonderful changing views of the surrounding hills. The walk is in the Teme Valley, and though we start alongside the Teme most of the route is close to its tributary the River Clun.

THE PUB The **Lion Hotel** has a beautiful location alongside the river, with a riverside garden; winter floods occasionally reach up to the door. Originally a coaching inn, parts of the pub date from 1740. In the 1840s it had a short spell as a theatre, associated with the Ludlow Theatre Company. The owner is

---

Distance – 4½ miles.

OS Explorer 203 Ludlow (start and end) and 201 Knighton and Presteigne; **Landranger** 137 Church Stretton and Ludlow. GR 403739.

Starting point The Lion Hotel by the river in Leintwardine.

How to get there Leintwardine is about 8 miles west of Ludlow on the road to Knighton, the A4113. Patrons may leave their cars at the pub (with permission) while walking. Alternatively, park at the community centre/library in the middle of the village.

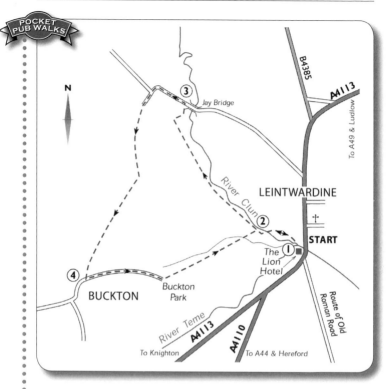

POCKET
PUB WALKS

N

Jay Bridge ③

River Clun

B4385

A4113

To A49 & Ludlow

LEINTWARDINE

②

†

START ①

The Lion Hotel

④

BUCKTON

Buckton Park

River Teme

A4113

A4110

Route of Old Roman Road

To Knighton

To A44 & Hereford

an award-winning chef, and the food provides evidence of this. Especially popular is the Sunday lunch. The selection of beers includes Theakston's, and a choice of lager and cider is also on tap.

☎ 01547 540203

[1] From the pub turn left and pass the post office, built on the site of the former Roman baths. Turn left along the narrow road by the garage. A footpath sign points this way as we pass **Water's Edge** and several other houses on our left, near the river bank. The surfaced driveway bends right up to **Seedley House**, but we

keep straight ahead along a muddy track. Reach a gate across the track, with signs telling us that this is a public footpath, vehicles are not allowed and there is no fishing without a permit. Continue along the drive, until we reach another gate, and turn left here.

2 Cross the footbridge alongside a cattle bridge over the **River Clun**, and turn right through a small gate to walk alongside the river. Enjoy the first of many good views to the surrounding hills – **Hopton Park** and **Bucknell Hill** are ahead, capped with trees. Go through a gate and follow the river bank, but at the next gate move away from the river to cross the middle of the field, following the direction of the arrow. Aim to the right of the house seen ahead. Walk on to reach another arrow, at the corner of a hedge, by a footbridge. Go right, over this unfenced footbridge, and then diagonally left across the next field. This takes us to a large gate, and a narrow road, by the **Jay Bridge**.

Jay House.

Herefordshire

3 Turn left along this road, walking alongside a ditch and a few willow trees, which are numerous in this flat and often wet landscape. When the road divides, the right fork is to **Bedstone**, but we take the left fork leading towards **Jay Farm**, which sits on a slight rise, above the wet ground. Pass to the right of the modernised **Jay Barn** and **Jay Farmhouse**, through a metal gate and along the track. Reach a gate and a bridge over the stream, then stay close to the fence along the left margin of a field. Ignore a crosspaths and keep straight ahead. Go through a gate and along the hedged grassy track, which we follow for about a mile. The houses of **Buckton** come into view ahead and slightly to the right, but at the T-junction we turn left.

4 Follow the narrow lane (or a parallel path, part of the **Herefordshire Trail** – just inside the field to the right) as far as the buildings of **Buckton Park**. Fork left off the driveway just before the buildings and go through a gate, then fork slightly left away from the buildings to a stile by another metal gate. Cross a small field, an old orchard, to a stile – with the buildings on our right. Then go across the next field slightly left of straight ahead, over a double stile and ditch in the hedge and across the next field. The church tower is nearly straight ahead, just protruding above the trees. Cross a large field, with a ditch to our right, to reach a footbridge and then cross another field to another footbridge. We have now reached point 2 again and we cross the cattle bridge over the **River Clun**, and turn right along the track to return to the starting point.

Places of interest nearby

Some 6 miles south-west of Ludlow is the romantic ruin of **Wigmore Castle**, once a stronghold of the Mortimer family. Now in the care of English Heritage, admission is free.